PEARLS THAT SOAK MY DRESS

Elegies for a Child

JAHAN MALEK KHATUN

Translated by
Dick Davis

MAGE PUBLISHERS

Copyright © 2021 Mage Publishers

All rights reserved. No part of this book may be reproduced or retransmitted in any manner whatsoever, except in the form of a review, without the written permission of the publisher.

Mage Publishers, Inc.
www.mage.com

Library of Congress Cataloging-in-Publication Data
Available at the Library of Congress

ISBN 978-1-949445-33-6

Email: as@mage.com
Mage online: www.mage.com

*To the Memory of
Mariam Darbandi, 1956–1983*

Contents

Introduction ix
Elegies

ONE	1
TWO	3
THREE	7
FOUR	9
FIVE	15
SIX	17
SEVEN	21
EIGHT	23
NINE	25
TEN	27
ELEVEN	29
TWELVE	31
THIRTEEN . . .	33
FOURTEEN . . .	35
FIFTEEN . . .	37
SIXTEEN . . .	39
SEVENTEEN . . .	41
EIGHTEEN . . .	43
NINETEEN . . .	45
TWENTY . . .	47
TWENTY-ONE . .	49
TWENTY-TWO . .	51
TWENTY-THREE . .	53

Introduction

Jahan Malek Khatun was a princess of the Inju family which ruled Shiraz and its environs in the first half of the fourteenth century. The Injus were a family of mixed Mongol-Persian heritage; the Mongol side was descended from Hulagu Khan, the grandson of Genghiz Khan, and the Persian side claimed descent from the eleventh-century Sufi poet Ansari. As was the custom in other tribal units descended from the thirteenth-century Mongol conquerors of Iran, noble Inju women took an active part in court life, and the fourteenth-century traveler Ibn Battuta implies that they routinely went unveiled; this relatively permissive state of affairs was probably a major enabling circumstance for Jahan Khatun's eventual emergence as both an admired poet and a significant presence in the life of the Inju court. Jahan Khatun's father, Masud Shah, was briefly the ruler of Shiraz until he was assassinated in 1342; his death was avenged by his brother, Jahan's uncle, Abu Es'haq, who ruled

Shiraz from 1343 to 1353 and had a reputation as a charismatic, amiable, pleasure-loving sovereign. He was also a major patron of poets (his court poets included the most famous poet of the age, Hafez, as well as lesser but still distinguished poets such as Khaju Kermani and Obayd-e Zakani) and his brief reign was seen as a golden age of poetry and courtly pleasure.

Jahan Khatun's parents married in 1324, and this gives us the earliest probable date for her birth; as her father was killed in 1342 she cannot have been more than a teenager when this happened, and she may have been much younger. As a young woman she seems to have held a cherished position at her uncle's court, a place where poetry was welcomed and highly valued, and it may well have been this pervasive atmosphere of poetic production that set her off on her own poetic career (though in the preface to her collected poems she admits that for a while she hesitated before beginning to write, giving as her reasons firstly that she was unsure of whether this would be a "proper" occupation for a young princess, and secondly that she doubted whether she possessed the necessary literary talent).

At some point, probably when she was in her teens or early twenties, Jahan Khatun married a fellow courtier at her uncle's court. Her husband's name was Amin al-Din Jahromi; he was her uncle's *nadim*, that is his drinking buddy and intimate confidant, the man with whom he could relax from royal duties and courtly protocol. Marriages involving royal personages tended to be made for political reasons and to cement alliances, but as a mark of special favor a king would sometimes give one of his daughters or nieces as a bride to a close friend, and this may well have been how Jahan Khatun's marriage to her uncle's convivial companion came about. If Amin al-Din Jahromi was more or less the same age as Jahan Khatun's uncle, as is likely, this would mean that he was probably at least twenty years older than Jahan, and perhaps much more than this. If Jahan's poems are to be believed the marriage was not a particularly happy one, and some of her poems hint that she was often left alone while her uncle and husband were off carousing somewhere.

All the carousing and the poetry came to an abrupt end in 1353 when Shiraz was overrun by the warlord Mobarez al-Din, and Abu Es'haq, and the other males in Jahan's family, were executed. If her husband was also killed at this time this would mean that Jahan was now a widow and so without any obvious means of support; some of her poems refer to a time in prison, and others to being exiled from Shiraz. Mobarez al-Din was renowned for both his piety and his brutality, and the daily life of Shiraz changed radically during his reign: public morality was strictly enforced, music and alcohol were forbidden, and the city's contemptuous inhabitants gave their new ruler a derisive nickname, "the morals officer." Five years after the conquest, even

Mobarez's own son, Shah Shoja, found his father's pious thuggishness insupportable and deposed him. He proved to be a much more easy-going ruler than his father had been; he soon relaxed his father's most draconian regulations and the city breathed a collective sigh of relief. Jahan Kahtun eventually made her peace with Shah Shoja and returned to Shiraz where she seems to have lived out the rest of her life unmolested and in relative obscurity. She died at some time after 1382, though exactly when is not known.

Anomalous though her situation may have been, and despite the initial uncertainty that she had mentioned in her preface to her *Divan* (Collected Poems) as to whether she should or even could write poetry at all, Jahan Khatun clearly came to see herself as a poet among other poets, and not in any sense as a lone eccentric outsider. It was (and to some extent still is) not uncommon for Persian language poets to include in a poem a line by a predecessor or a contemporary whose poetry they especially admired (the practice was referred to as a "welcoming" of the venerated figure into one's own work), and Jahan Khatun does this with a line in one of her poems from Sa'di, which she introduces with her own line, "As is customary, I introduce (into my poem) this beautiful line / by Sheikh (Sa'di) whose poetic talent my soul reveres." Sa'di was the great poet of Shiraz from the previous century (he died some thirty years before Jahan Khatun's birth), famous for the limpid elegance of his lyric verse, and for, as it was called, the "difficult simplicity" of his diction. Given Jahan Khatun's "welcoming" of Sa'di, it is not surprising that much of her verse evidently aims at a Sa'di-like elegance rather than complexity, and at simplicity of statement rather than allusive ambiguity (such as we find in, for example, the poetry of Jahan Khatun's contemporary and fellow courtier, Hafez). But she was not a figure locked in the poetic past, since she was clearly aware of the court poets around her; she echoes phrases by her much older contemporary Khaju Kermani occasionally, and she quite often echoes phrases and sentiments from Hafez's poems. It's been assumed that a major poet like Hafez would not be interested in alluding to the verse of a local princess who was still relatively unknown outside of her uncle's court, and that Jahan Khatun must be echoing Hafez rather than the other way round. But it would have been a shrewd political move for a courtier-poet like Hafez to refer to the poems of a princess who was also the favored niece of the patron on whose largesse he depended, and it's possible that sometimes the great man is alluding to a line by the princess, rather than vice-versa.

Although most of Jahan Khatun's poems (the exceptions were usually poems about politics and public affairs) were written according to an aesthetic of elegant simplicity, this doesn't mean that they avoid the conventional strategies of medieval Persian poetic rhetoric, and some of these strategies will inevitably appear strange, "unnatural" even, for an audience that is not used to them. The most obvious difference from western poetry of the same and later periods is that most Persian poets of the medieval period show virtually no interest in original (and therefore new) metaphors; the arsenal of metaphors thought to be suitable for poetry was considered to be available to everyone and was universally used as a matter of course. Also, a strategy that is quite common in a great deal of western poetry from the same period but is not utilized nearly to the extent that Persian poets utilized it, is that virtually all descriptions (whether of people, landscapes, emotional states, or anything else), tend to move immediately to the hyperbolic and, in literal terms at least, incredible; this is particularly true of lyric poetry. A good example of hyperbole that incorporates the incredible is the title of this book, *Pearls That Soak My Dress*. This metaphor sounds peculiar in English for the obvious reason that pearls can't soak anything; that is, the metaphor states something incredible / impossible. But of course the "pearls" here are tears, which can soak something. The incredible aspect of the metaphor is a major part of what makes it "work" in Persian. Another example that very often crops up in medieval Persian poetry is when someone is described as a "walking cypress tree"; again, in English, this is an impossibility (cypress trees don't walk anywhere), but "cypress tree" is a common metaphor in Persian poetry for a young slim beautiful person, and like the "pearls" soaking a dress, the "cypress tree" is able to walk.

A particularly difficult example, at least for some western readers, of such hyperbole is the expression "tears of blood" or "bloody tears." Tears are virtually always characterized in Persian poetry as red (the almost sole exception is when they are compared to pearls), and this is because it is blood, or blood and tears together, that is being shed. This is in fact a real condition (called haemolacria) brought on by excessive weeping, and it is exactly this excessiveness that is being implied when the phrase occurs in Persian poetry. But although the phrase turns up in other cultures (Chaucer's Troilus says that his heart weeps "blody teris," and in Book XVI of the *Iliad* Zeus weeps "tears of blood" for the death of Sarpedon), its omnipresence in Persian poetry goes far beyond western instances of the phenomenon. It's also possible that something else is going on in the phrase: "blood" is sometimes used in Persian as a metaphor for suffering; for example "to drink blood" means to suffer with little hope of redress. Though the metaphor was most common in the medieval period it has survived to the present day (in one of her poems the twentieth-century poet Parvin Etesami has an orphaned child say, "Luck's stream is milk, they say; when I went there / To drink from it, blood was my scalding share").

"Tears of blood" could therefore be understood to mean "tears of suffering"; that said, the frequent insistence on the red color of the tears indicates that the blood is also being conceived of literally. Though the metaphorical meaning of "blood" ("suffering") may reinforce the literal meaning it does not replace it.

Given the number of disastrous events that Jahan lived through — her father's murder when she was a teenager and eleven years later the execution of her male relatives including the uncle who had taken her under his wing after her father's death, the annihilation of her family's royal power, her imprisonment for a while and her exile (to both of which a few of her poems refer), and also given her probably unsatisfactory marriage — it's a little surprising that Jahan Khatun still comes across in her poems as a woman who was always remarkably ready to enjoy life whenever the opportunities to do so appeared, and to relish as much as she could the pleasures within her grasp. She remembers with nostalgic affection the girlish fun she shared with the friends of her youth, she delights in celebratory open-air events like court picnics, her love of gardens is conventional for poets of her period but even so her appreciative response to their beauty can often seem personal rather than predictably "poetic," and it seems that whenever it is possible she grasps at erotic pleasure with unabashed enthusiasm. Knowing nothing of her actual history a reader who skimmed through her *divan* could well believe that she lived a life of almost unalloyed privilege and pleasure. That is, until this reader reached a short section near the end of the divan labelled "*Marsiyeh*," "Elegies." Even a quick skim through these reveals a woman whose heart has been broken and whose virtually constant emotional state is one of despair.

These elegies (there are twenty-three of them) are all for one person, her daughter Soltan Bakht who died at a very young age, probably when she was either still a babe in arms or a toddler. Jahan Khatun had a step-mother who was also named Soltan Bakht and to whom she was apparently very close, and because of this it was sometimes assumed that the elegies were for this Soltan Bakht, but whoever first suggested this cannot have seen the manuscript in which it is unequivocally stated that these elegies are for her child ("*farzand*"), and it's also clear from the occasional details within the elegies themselves that the person referred to is a very young child. It seems likely that Jahan Khatun named her daughter Soltan Bakht as a gesture of respect and affection for the stepmother who had befriended her.

The poems themselves provide eloquent evidence for the paramount importance Jahan attached to her daughter's death, but even more telling is the fact that she returned to the subject so many times; other adverse events, both personal and political, that happened to her are mentioned in her poems a few times, but none receive such obsessive attention as that which she gave to the loss of her infant daughter. Like all her poems (and like all poems written by all Persian court poets at this time) her elegies are written firmly within the courtly poetic conventions of their time, but there is no mistaking the rawness of emotion out of which the poems have arisen. An emphasis on elegance of tone and form, and on artificiality of diction, might suggest that the emotional force of poems written in this manner must be very muted, or even perhaps that there is no emotional force to be discovered there at all, that the poems are all form and no substance, but this is very far from the case.

A comparison with an approximately contemporary elegy for a young girl, this time one written in England, should make this clear. The very beautiful anonymous fourteenth-century poem *Pearl*, in which a father laments the death of his two year old daughter (the "Pearl" of the title), is written with a high degree of sophisticated rhetorical complexity, and yet the paternal grief expressed throughout the poem (but especially at its opening) is palpable; indeed, we can say that it is this very rhetorical complexity that makes it palpable. The poem begins as a straightforward lament but quickly turns into a dream vision, in which the dreamer is theologically instructed by his dead daughter (whom he sees on the other side of a stream he cannot cross) in order that he be reconciled to her death. The poem is clearly strongly influenced by Dante's *Commedia*, especially the *Paradiso*, with the little girl more or less taking on the role of an infant Beatrice as she explains to the writer the nature of heaven, so that as the poem proceeds the father's grief is as it were gradually sublimated by and into theology. None of Jahan Khatun's elegies involve an interlocutor and the persistent grief in them stays wholly immediate, personal, and unresolved. The narrative element in *Pearl*, and the back and forth exchanges between father and daughter, make emotional modification and development possible, but in each of the separate elegies by Jahan Khatun we see her starting from the same emotionally unvarying place. In *Pearl* the father is removed from the immediacy of his grief by a dream vision in which he quickly turns his eyes to heaven, where his daughter now exists, and where the poem remains for the rest of its course; Jahan Khatun twice (elegies 10 and 16) refers to her certainty that her daughter is now in heaven, but she doesn't develop this notion; likewise, in three of her elegies (4, 6 and 7) she turns to God, but there is no sense that this in any way mitigates her grief, which remains simply that – grief, pure and simple, repeatedly referred to with seemingly unending regret.

A few of these poems have appeared in previously published books (*Faces of Love: Hafez and the Poets of Shiraz*, 2012, 2013, and *The Mirror of My Heart, a Thousand Years of Persian Poetry by Women*, 2019, 2021), and on the strength of these examples Dr. Sarah McNamer of Georgetown University was kind enough to suggest to me that it might be useful to non-Persian speakers if I translated all of Jahan Khatun's elegies for her daughter. I am very grateful to her for this suggestion, as without her generous encouragement this little book would almost certainly not exist.

*Elegies for her beloved child Soltan Bakht;
may her dust be fragrant**

---

* "May her dust be fragrant," a conventional phrase when mentioning the dead

ONE

What pain, what sorrow, that my soul's
　delight has gone
So young that sweet soul was, and from the
　world* she's gone

A loving heart, your face the full moon – to
　what end?
In longing for that face my very soul has gone.

Go, tell the garden's nightingale to sing no
　more –
Since from the garden's flowers that flower-
　like face has gone;

My heart, when will you reach to where loved
　souls abide
Since her dear soul's tracked down Death's
　caravan, and gone.

---

* The Persian word for "world" is "*Jahan,*" which is of course one of Jahan Khatun's names. Almost every time that this word occurs in these elegies a pun is involved, so that, for example, here "and from the world she's gone" also means "and from Jahan (i.e. from me) she's gone."

How I complain, how I beseech the
  seven heavens
And how my tears pour down … until they
  too have gone;

My Soltan Bakht sat here enthroned by our
  shared love
Oh why should my unlucky stars decree
  she's gone?

Light of my eyes, my grief for you destroys
  Jahan
Since you who were their light have left the
  world, and gone

What sorrow and what grief Jahan takes from
  this world
And weak with grief belongs in neither world,
  she's gone.†

---

† "she's" refers to Jahan Khatun herself; she is saying that her grief has meant that she exists in a state that is neither alive (in this world), nor dead (in the world after death).

TWO

O heart and eyes, my heart and eyes
   suffused with blood,
My soul is seared with grief too dreadful
   to confess –

From heaven's cruelty my damp eyes drip
   tears of blood*
And absence turns them to an Oxus
   of distress.

My kindly friends all seek to comfort me;
   they say,
" Poor wretch, how can you cope with
   such unhappiness?"

But given all that I've endured, what can
   I say?
You know my grief's a grief mere words
   cannot express.

---

* "tears of blood": see Introduction, pp. xv–xvi.

Let heaven boast, not me, I shan't complain
  aloud;
Your rose-like face is buried, and there's
  no redress.

I weep though; now I'll never see your
  lovely face
My face is smeared with flowing tears I
  can't suppress.

Where has the Layli of my soul now gone?
  Tell me –
Jahan's become Majnun,† lost in his
  wilderness!

---

† Layli and Majnun are the archetypal lovers of Persian (and Middle Eastern generally) literature. Majnun's separation from Layli sends him mad and he flees from mankind to live alone in the wilderness; Jahan is living in a "wilderness" of grief caused by her separation from her child, who is being compared to Layli. Layli and Majnun are often used as analogies or metaphors in erotic verse, but this is not exclusively the case; here the love involved is between a mother and her daughter, and Layli and Majun are invoked because of the intensity of grief that separation from the loved person brings.

My heart, my sweet life's ending bitterly;
   I suffer,
Hoping to ease your suffering through
   my faithfulness;[‡]

My lot is torment in this wretched world,
Bent with unalterable unhappiness.

[‡] This obliquely refers to the belief that by suffering with or on behalf of someone, that person's suffering is to that extent relieved; the European proverb, "a sorrow shared is a sorrow halved" expresses the same notion.

THREE

In Jahan's garden now the rose's face is hidden,
            her petals have departed –
They've left the lovelorn nightingale to sing
            alone and brokenhearted

That rose once smiled within the garden of my hope –
            injustice now has left
Your thorn of absence in my grieving soul
            and I am here bereft

Luck turned her back on me the moment that
            you slipped away from me
And since that day of your departure I
            live lost in misery

It's not for me to be beside you, or to know
            such sweetness and delight,
Since destiny's against me and has hidden you
            in exile's endless night

And now what untoward, strange circumstance is this –
            since people rightly say,
"How could it be that dust and dirt should hide the sun's
            resplendent face away"?

My cries rise up into the heavens, but what use
                is my lamenting voice?
Tell me, apart from patience what is there for me,
                since I've no other choice?

All of the doctors in the world cannot produce
                a medicine that will heal
The wretchedness your endless absence gives to me,
                or soothe the pain I feel.

What miseries the heavens have rained on me, and yet
                many I can control –
The absence of my friends has wounded my poor heart,
                your absence wounds my soul.

FOUR

Your absence is a fire from which
    black, choking vapors rise
A thousand streams of blood and tears
    flow from my weeping eyes
How cruelly have the scornful heavens
    tormented and abused me
Now that once more my wretched fate
    has blinded me and bruised me
I swear upon my darlings' dust,
    that since my mother bore me
My eyes see nothing but
    disasters rising up before me
What have I seen the world bestow
    on me but misery,
Since not an instant's happiness
    was ever granted me?
A moment snatched from me
    my patience, self-control, and peace,
And every moment saw
    the anguish in my heart increase
Jahan's unhappy soul, the world
    itself, was seared with grief,

And all who saw me thought they'd grant
    my aching heart relief
But those I gave my heart to
    burned it with yet more pain
And when I looked for their support
    I found I looked in vain
How can I tell what I've endured?
    who's borne what I've been through?
Who's seen such days, or heard
    of such misfortune? Tell me, who?
The wind of nothingness has snatched
    my rose from me, and I
Feel grief's thorn tearing at my soul
    as strength and patience die
Misfortune's been my fortune since
    the day that I was born,
Its face is stained with suffering's blood
    and all I do is mourn
Light of my eyes, my Soltan Bakht,
    the like of your dear face
Was never known at any time
    or glimpsed in any place
Her absence is the brand that maims
    Jahan's poor soul: "Goodbye"
She said, and left me weeping tears
    of blood that she should die

Fate snatched her from the world, and threw
    her into Death's abyss,
Alas that silver limbs, her rose-like face,
    should come to this!
Not for an instant was her lot
    to live in happiness
Not for a moment was her mind
    untarnished by distress
Her spiteful fate ensured she saw
    no loving purity
In all her life no moment passed
    in safe security
Hail to you, faithless Fate,
    compounded of deceit and lies!
Tell me, what's your fell purpose here,
    if not to terrorize?
No love shone from the heaven's face
    as though it were the sun,
Mercy did not touch broken hearts
    that sorrow had undone
What elegant narcissus, tended
    with heartfelt care,
Is not cut down in due course by
    the sickle of despair?
And what tall cypress we've rejoiced
    to see securely grow,

Does not succumb when Fate's saw
      furiously lays it low?
My doctor's counsel, and my kindly
      friends' advice agree,
"Patience is what you need, since there's
      no other remedy".
A voice came to me from the heavens,
      "O desperate nightingale,
It's Fate that stole your rose… and tears
      will be of no avail".
Almighty Lord, to whose commands
      your abject slaves must bow,
Grant me exceeding patience
      in my affliction now
Fate snatched my soul's companion from
      my arms, and in her leaving
All pleasures in the world bade me
      farewell, and left me grieving
But if pain plucks me like a harp
      that cries a thousand cries,
Or if like sandalwood I burn
      in sorrows' tears and sighs
You are my Lord and as your slave
      I patiently
Resign my soul and being to the path
      You've given me

Whatever earthly mold a soul
        from heaven might take on
It must be parted from that mold
        once mortal life has gone
If it's the head You seek, the head's
        Your sacrificial due,
And if You snatch away the soul
        the soul belongs to You
Be merciful to me, O Lord,
        forgiving and benign,
Though I've no hope that happiness
        can once again be mine
This weight of sin upon my wretched heart,
        may it suffice –
And may the troubles of my life here end
        in paradise!
Sinful and guilty though I am, I wait
        at Your court's entrance
Hoping that I shan't be excluded from
        Your loving presence
And if the world won't pity me I shan't
        seek here for solace
All that I long for now is You, Your presence
        And Your grace.

FIVE

Your heart a rose-bush, and your soul a cypress,
   Sweet pleasure's bud, fruit worthy of the spirit,
And I a mother now without her child
   Denied life's joy, and all life should inherit

How men loved seeing what they'd never seen
   Till – like a fairy's child – she slipped from sight;
Don't criticize me when I weep, but think
   How Jacob wept for Joseph day and night.

What wound is this, whose only balm is tears?
   What pain, whose cure's lamenting and distress?
I weep a flowing river, and Oman
   Has never seen these pearls that soak my dress.

While I have eyes within my head, and while
   My tongue is in my mouth, I'll always see
Her image in my eyes, and on my tongue
   Her name will be repeated endlessly.

This grief's so scorched my heart that when I'm dust
   That dust will show my sorrow all too well;
My house that was a shining paradise
   Is darker now than any dungeon cell

My heart was like a home that welcomed pleasure,
  Now only grief comes knocking at its door;
My suffering heart has borne so much it's like
  A storm-tossed boat that cannot reach the shore.

Prepare to leave this temporary hovel,*
  When autumn comes the nightingales are leaving;
It's Fate that heaps these sorrows on our heads,
  And Time is not to blame when we are grieving.†

---

* "temporary hovel": the world.

† The last lines mean, "What happens is not a result of time's vicissitudes but has been fated from eternity."

SIX

What pain is there the heavens haven't given me,
What sorrow by which Fate has not yet
 driven me?
What longing have I not endured, what
 dreadful fears
Have not imbrued my soul's face with these
 blood-soaked tears?*
What cypress† was it that I glimpsed before it
 fled
Whose absence now provokes the blood and
 tears I shed ?
What have I done that this should be
 my punishment?

---

* "these blood soaked tears": see Introduction, pp. xv–xvi.

† The cypress tree is a conventional metaphor for a beautiful young person (usually an adolescent, but here Jahan Khatun's child). Like most epithets describing a loved person "cypress" can be used for both men and women. It's worth noting that the beloved in Persian poetry tends to be of indeterminate sex and it is usually difficult to tell whether a poem's subject is a boy or a girl. Persian grammar can add to this ambiguity, as there are virtually no gender markers in the language and the same word is used for both "he" and "she."

Is bad luck always mine, my sorrow heaven-
 sent?
My lovely Layli left me here, and then how
 soon
The torment of her absence made me
 like Majnun!‡
Her absence is a snake that bites the heart,
 and for
The mortal wound it makes don't think there
 is a cure,
Or think my tears could drown my heart's
 unruly fire
When all that they can do is make the flames
 beat higher.
You see my silver tears stain golden cheeks
 as though,
My soul, they didn't care about the wounds
 below –
Jahan burns up with pain, and questions
 everyone
"Ah when will this atrocious agony be done"?
But then she says, "May no one ever be
 like me,
Friendless, with such a fate, bowed down
 by misery;

---

‡ Layli and Majnun: see note on page 4.

My hope is for God's mercy, that I'll
 live within
His grace, and be delivered from the fires
 of sin".

SEVEN

O God, I beg you, open wide
    The gates of heaven
For one to whom a heavenly nature
    Had been given;

Grant her a place in paradise,
    And may the throngs
Of lovely angels welcome her
    Where she belongs;

Keep far from her this world's desires,
    Its grief and spite;
Bestow your grace on her, and fill
    Her soul with light.

EIGHT

Now may her goodness be a guide
    to those who follow
The footsteps of one taken from
    the world in sorrow;

Don't scatter roses on the grave
    in which she lies
Since up into the highest heaven
    her pure soul flies –

And in her heart may worldly memories
    leave no trace,
May musk and ambergris be found there,
    in their place.

NINE

The heavens have left my mind confused and desolate –
O God, may no one ever live in my sad state!
My choking sobs are endless, but I clearly say,
"My dearest friends, Alas for Soltan Bakht's cruel fate"!

TEN

If in her face this world has slammed its door,
And if its thorns have rendered her foot-sore
She sits in paradise with angels now –
I don't think this, I *know* it's so, I'm sure.

ELEVEN

The arrow of your absence struck my soul
                and made it yield,
Its point had pierced my heart, which I had thought
                would be my shield –
And when he saw the wound my doctor said
                "There is no hope –
No balm could sooth an injury like this,
                it can't be healed".

TWELVE

O heaven, how long will your
 injustice to my soul go on?
Shame on you for my wounded heart
 that's left me woebegone,
Not for a moment do you think
 to give me all I long for,
And never has my soul rejoiced
 in anything you've done.

THIRTEEN

A painter keeps a tulip's image in his mind
And from its form his painting's image is designed –
The form Jahan is seeking's bade the world goodbye
And now she has concealed herself from all mankind.

FOURTEEN

How long will heaven sew for me
        these garments of despair?
Look at me well, and in my heart
        see sorrow's fiery glare –
But how could words describe the wasteland
        of my wretched heart
Now that misfortune's cruelty heaps up
        sorrow everywhere?

FIFTEEN

My soul's on fire with grief again. "My soul" I say,
When all Jahan is burning in the same sad way ...
The heart can burn, and still the soul might stay concealed –
But I can see my life and being burn away.

Though I've been harried by the turning skies
That stole my rose despite my anguished cries,
I saw the gate to Rezvan's garden* open
And glimpsed her face there with my wondering eyes.

---

* Rezvan's garden is paradise; Rezvan is the angel who guards paradise.

SEVENTEEN

Each new flower opening in the morning light,
Filling my heart with glory and delight . . .
Even before its perfume reaches me
Destruction's wind has swept it from my sight.

EIGHTEEN

Since first she shunned my presence, it was plain
She'd rather leave me heartsick than remain;
She took no pity on her soul or me
But left her mother here, to sigh in vain.

NINETEEN

My noble child, since you have gone,
   my wretched mind
Feels so disordered and distressed
   and undermined ...
And you who know such things, how long
   should sleep go on for?
Come on my dear, wake up now, leave this
   sleep behind.*

---

* The poem is ambiguous; the last line could refer to Soltan Bakht (Jahan is telling her child to "wake up" from the sleep of death) or it could refer to Jahan Khatun herself (she is telling herself to wake up from her "dream" that she can be in touch with her dead child). The first interpretation, which is the primary one, indicates that she is still nursing the illusion that her child can somehow be returned to her; the second has almost the opposite implication, that she is telling herself to "wake up" from the illusion that she can communicate with her child, or that she might somehow be reunited with her.

TWENTY

However many kings the world brings down to dust
They were the world's and loved the world they leave;
My Soltan Bakht's destroyed both worlds,* and left
Jahan to burn within her inmost being and to grieve.

---

* "both world's": this world and the world after death. "Soltan Bakht's destroyed both worlds" means that she has made this world and heaven non-existent for me, nothing to me.

Not for a moment will your absence let me rest,
Not for a minute will the heavens let me sleep;
The light has left my grieving eyes forever now
And from them it's no longer tears but blood I weep.

TWENTY-TWO

My heart will take no drug to dull this pain,
The seal of sorrow's set, and will remain:
My heart could never tire of your sweet presence,
Absence is all my life can now contain.

TWENTY-THREE

My heart is bowed with grief now that you've gone,
And it is tears of blood my poor eyes shed;
Your face was both my sun and moon, and in
Their absence tears have stained my face rose-red.*

---

* "...rose-red" i.e. with tears of blood. See Introduction.
pp. xv–xvi.

Other Mage Poetry Titles

Faces of Love: Hafez and the Poets of Shiraz
Bilingual Edition / Translated by Dick Davis

*The Mirror of My Heart:
A Thousand Years of Persian Poetry by Women*
Bilingual Edition / Translated by Dick Davis

Layli and Majnun
Nezami Ganjavi / Translated by Dick Davis

Vis and Ramin
Fakhraddin Gorgani / Translated by Dick Davis

Shahnameh: The Persian Book of Kings
Abolqasem Ferdowsi / Translated by Dick Davis

Rostam: Tales of Love and War from Persia's Book of Kings
Abolqasem Ferdowsi / Translated by Dick Davis

Borrowed Ware: Medieval Persian Epigrams
Introduced and Translated by Dick Davis

When They Broke Down the Door: Poems
Fatemeh Shams / Introduction and translations by Dick Davis

Milkvetch and Violets
Mohammad Reza Shafi'i Kadkani / translated by Mojdeh Bahar

Another Birth and Other Poems
By Forugh Farrokhzad, translated by Hasan Javadi
and Susan Sallée / Bilingual edition

Obeyd-e Zakani: Ethics of Aristocrats and other Satirical Works
translated by Hasan Javadi

Audio Books

Faces of Love: Hafez and the Poets of Shiraz
Translated by Dick Davis / Penguin Audio / Read by
Dick Davis, Tala Ashe and Ramiz Monsef

The Mirror of My Heart:
A Thousand Years of Persian Poetry by Women
Translated by Dick Davis / Penguin Audio / Read by
Dick Davis, Mozhan Marno, Tala Ashe and Serena Manteghi

Layli and Majnun
Nezami Ganjavi / Translated by Dick Davis
Penguin Audio / Read by
Dick Davis, Peter Ganim, Serena Manteghi and Sean Rohani

Vis and Ramin
Fakhraddin Gorgani / Translated by Dick Davis
Mage Audio / Read by
Mary Sarah Agliotta, Dick Davis (introduction)

My Uncle Napoleon
Iraj Pezeshkzad / Translated by Dick Davis
Mage Audio / Read by
Moti Margolin, Dick Davis (introduction)

Savushun: A Novel about Modern Iran
Simin Daneshvar / Translated by M.R. Ghanoonparvar
Mage Audio / Read by
Mary Sarah Agliotta, Brian Spooner (introduction)

Crowning Anguish: Taj al-Saltana
Memoirs of a Persian Princess
from the Harem to Modernity, 1884–1914
Introduction by Abbas Amanat / Translated by Anna Vanzan
Mage Audio / Read by
Kathreen Khavari

www.ingramcontent.com/pod-product-compliance
Lightning Source LLC
Chambersburg PA
CBHW030057170426
43197CB00010B/1555